Mary X~

_

c

2019.

Donato Cinicolo is a professional photographer, but has always been keen on making things with his hands. He was born in Italy in a small Appeninean village, and even at an early age he used to 'knock up' toys using scrap wood. Later Donato lived in a seventeenth-century building that required a lot of maintenance, so he had to learn traditional skills like wattle-and-daub plastering. It proved to be both enjoyable and very satisfying, so much so that neighbours began asking Donato to build them a bespoke little building. Most of the techniques employed are traditional carpentry skills, mixed with some foraging (it's always better getting stuff for nothing). To date, Donato has made over a dozen sheds, three of which are in his own back garden. In fact this book has been written in one of them!

Also by Donato Cinicolo
Me and My Bike: Portraits of a Cycling Nation

MY SHED
AND HOW IT WAS BUILT

A How To Book

Donato Cinicolo

ROBINSON

ROBINSON

First published in Great Britain in 2015 by Robinson

Copyright © Donato Cinicolo, 2015

The moral right of the author has been asserted.

A CIP catalogue record for this book
is available from the British Library.

ISBN 978-1-84528-550-0 (hardback)
ISBN: 978-1-84528-563-0 (ebook)

Typeset in Great Britain by Ian Hughes, www.mousematdesign.com
Printed and bound in China by C&C Offset Printing Co. Ltd

Robinson
is an imprint of
Constable & Robinson Ltd
100 Victoria Embankment
London EC4Y 0DY

An Hachette UK Company
www.hachette.co.uk

www.constablerobinson.com

How To Books are published by Constable & Robinson, a part of Little, Brown
Book Group. We welcome proposals from authors who have first-hand experience
of their subjects. Please set out the aims of your book, its target market and its
suggested contents in an email to Nikki.Read@howtobooks.co.uk

CONTENTS

INTRODUCTION

'Shed' is a wonderful four-letter word: everyone seems to understand its meaning, but it's difficult to pin down a definition of a shed. To some it's a garden store; to others it's a refuge from the world, from children, and so on. In my own garden I have three sheds, all built by me for different purposes. My tool shed houses tools, nails, screws and the like. The garden shed has gardening implements mostly, plus some climbing gear; it is made of wattle and daub with oak limbs for a frame. My main shed is brick-built under a leaden roof (I'd never made a lead roof so I wanted to have a go).

In researching material for this book, I met some eccentric and delightful 'sheddies'. It's always difficult for people to allow a stranger into their private world, much less a photographer. My passport to gaining trust was to carry a photograph which showed me making my wattle and daub shed. This image immediately convinced people that I was a true and faithful 'sheddy' and we immediately had a rapport.

I had a few failures, but in the main shed owners liked to talk about their sheds; how they scavenged wood from skips; how the door was found at the local dump; how the roof had been made from old printing plates, etc. I did manage to contact a violin maker who made his instruments in his shed, so I was desperate to include his shed in the book. I met him on his doorstep, but he wouldn't allow me to see his shed. Tantalisingly, he showed me a violin he'd made: it bore the number 185. 'Does that mean that you have made 185 violins?' I asked. 'Oh no,' he said. 'It's well over 200 by now!' But I never got to see his shed, and was left wondering what might have been.

I would like to record my most grateful thanks to everyone who gave me their time, and their permission to use the photographs and text. In addition, thanks must go to my son Leo (also a photographer in his own right) for his assistance in getting the best out of each digital photograph. He is also learning to build and love sheds!

Donato Cinicolo

THE CHALET

Several years ago, when Neil's two boys Toby and Christopher were in their mid-teens, the family home became rather crowded with friends and school chums wanting to come round and play music. It was decided that a solution might be to build a shed in the garden for the boys to entertain their friends without causing chaos in the home.

According to Neil, 'The situation just had to change. It was so crowded that we felt we were being eased out of our own house by gangs of teenagers. It was obvious that the boys needed a space of their own, so they could have fun without impinging on the rest of the house. We knew that when the shed was built it would always have "stuff" in it such as a TV and the usual detritus of boys' bedrooms – bikes and all the rest of it.'

Big enough to allow the occasional sleepover, the shed became the envy of many of their friends and the two boys spent most of their waking hours in there. That was about seven years ago. Since then, Christopher has moved away but Toby virtually lives in the shed most of the time. He likes the isolation, and the peace and quiet away from sounds of traffic or domesticity.

The name 'The Chalet' was originally suggested by friends as a joke. Later, Neil put up a poster of a view of the Swiss Alps on one wall. Eventually the poster acquired a frame of sorts, thus becoming a 'window' with a view. The Chalet it was.

Lately, the shed has had a new occasional visitor; a friend of Neil's, a police officer who comes to stay when he has early shifts to contend with. The Chalet's new guest is, of course, quiet, well-behaved and a model of good manners.

The frame is made of tanalised timber, heavily insulated with Rockwool. The outside cladding is of 150 mm, feather-edge, treated boards while the interior is made of wooden paneling which allows screws and shelves to be put up easily. The whole building rests on a concrete paved surface which is easy to keep clean.

The roof sits on timber trusses which in turn have tongue-and-groove boards fixed to them to provide a finished surface for the ceiling. Above the tongue-and-groove ceiling there is high-density foam insulation finished with marine plywood, so that the roof is actually quite well insulated. In order to keep expense down, the roof is covered in roofing felt, but this is split up into several 'trays' which keep the buckling normally associated with felt roofs to a minimum. The outside of the ridge is lead-covered since it offers better protection against frost and snow than simple felt.

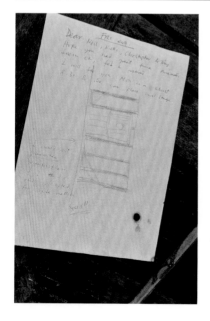

A stable door was made especially for the shed. The upper part has an opening porthole which was bought from a yacht chandlers in Shaftesbury Avenue in London. Small boys love to stick their heads through this unusual feature!

The windows were made on site to suit the building. They are simple and easy to maintain. One attractive feature is the projecting bay window, which houses a bed-platform with an excellent view of the garden. Everyone who visits loves to lie down in this space. Underneath the platform there is a huge space used for storage.

On one wall there is a view of the Swiss Alps, whilst on the opposite wall, on the lower part of the stable door, there is a poster of a roaring log fire. That way one can feel hot or cold, depending on which wall is viewed.

SHED OF SHAME

The strange name 'Shed of Shame' originates from when Ari's surveyor took one look at the building and immediately condemned it, as the roof had caved in and it was on the point of collapse. Ari and her husband were about to buy the house – they loved the location and the garden – but the shed, it was decided, had to be demolished. The view from the kitchen window was ruined by the derelict building.

However, Ari decided to call it The Shed of Shame, the idea coming from the film *Despicable Me,* and after a brief consultation with her local craftsman, it was agreed that the shed would be repaired.

Ari says 'I use the shed for absolutely everything. It's a laundry and drying area; it houses the additional fridge and freezer; I keep gardening stuff which I need all the time in there; excess cat food supplies [she is a cat lover]; china ornaments and wine. I only allow my husband Tony in there if he's good!' She uses the shed every day and is very happy that she kept the building.

Part of Ari's ancestry goes back to early medieval Florence, in Italy. She has a Mediterranean outlook and loves bright colours, ornamental china and flowers. That's why the shed was painted blue – to remind her of her Italian influence. Whenever her friends come round they all remark on the beauty of her shed. It was suggested that its name be changed, but to this day it has not happened.

The walls are of single-skin brick with piers, built around 1910. The inside surface has been cleaned and painted. The outside surface was in poor condition so Ari and Tony decided to render and paint the exterior after a few repairs were made.

The original roof had long since gone and been replaced by plastic. That, too, had succumbed to a mass of ivy invading from next door. Once the plastic and ivy had been removed, new tanalised rafters were put in. On top of that came tongue-and-groove boards which were then covered in areas of flat mineral felt. The edges of the roof were finished with 'flashband' which is a lead-covered, bituminous material. It makes a neat edge where the wind can't whip underneath (felt does not do well when it's bent over as it tends to crack at those points). Additionally, the roof surface was sub-divided into small areas which then had tanalised batten upstands added to cover joints and minimize large area contraction and expansion, which can lead to felt buckling.

There was only one window: which had been replaced a few decades ago. It was in good condition so it only needed painting. Ari has added a sign to amuse her friends. 'Laundry – drop your pants here!'

The floor is of brick in the original herringbone pattern and had several coverings when work began, including old lino (which stopped the brick from breathing) and a separate, floating chipboard floor. When all of this was removed the original bricks, which had been quite damp, dried out pretty quickly.

Part of Ari's ancestry includes the Pazzi family of Florence. The craftsman working on the building added a delightful flourish: the Pazzi coat of arms painted on an inside wall.

The door was a bit rotten but it was repaired and painted. A small porch was added to keep rainwater out of the top of the door. The threshold sill has had an old printing plate fixed over it to keep water out.

The outside walls have many personal touches such as china pots and figures, which all add to the individuality of this charming shed.

APPLE SHED

David is a gardener by profession. Almost by definition, he must have a shed – and so he has. Next to the building is an old, deformed apple tree, probably about half a century old or more. The trunk was rotten and split, but the remaining limbs still grew well and produced fruit. David could have cut it down and removed the trunk, but the tree was there first so the shed had to be built to accommodate it. Luckily there was a hard standing already there and the building sits on this alongside the tree.

About three years ago David bought the shed and had it put up. The building is very strong by small shed standards, as David wanted it to last a long time and not to have to continually keep up with repairs. Years ago, he had another shed, on an allotment. But when he gave up the plot he left the shed behind for the next incumbent.

David is very proud of his work benches. One cost 50p and the other was donated for nothing, including the vice. Both work surfaces are used most days, either to prepare plants for planting or to maintain tools. Most of the building provides safe, strong storage space. He does not allow many people into the shed 'because they might trip over something and cut themselves' as the space is quite small and congested.

David at work in his shed

This is a paved area on which timber bearers have been fixed to take the base of the shed. The old apple tree was cut only as absolutely necessary.

The timber frame uses shiplap, treated timber boards, as cladding. These are thicker and much stronger than the usual feather-edge boards used for sheds. The structure is inherently stiff and strong.

The felt roof is very simple and typical of most small sheds. It does the job but needs replacing every 10–20 years.

There are a couple of windows, to which David has added some basic curtains. It is important to have natural light when working at a bench.

The timber door is a basic braced and ledged frame with shiplap boards. The tee-hinges are, unusually for a shed, galvanized and thus need no maintenance apart from occasional oiling.

One of the delightful touches on this shed is the creeper, which David has allowed to go along the building and over the door; every time the door is opened the creeper stem has to bend like a hinge. It doesn't seem to mind.

WITT'S END

Grazia has had her shed for about twenty-five years. Her husband originally built it as a refuge from the noise of family life, pets and so on. It was designed to look like a Swiss chalet, with a porch and balustrading, and the idea was to keep logs under the covered part. The interior was wallpapered and a radiator fitted so that it looked and felt warm and cosy. The building was used as a den where you could escape to watch a film; to read; and even, before the introduction of digital photography, to develop photographs. Gradually, however, as children grew up and moved out the building became less and less used. Grazia says, 'One of these days I'll clear it out of all the junk and make it cosy again. When visitors come, sometimes their children like to play hide and seek, so it's a cool retreat.'

The Swiss chalet theme seems at odds with Grazia's Italian background, until you learn that some of her relatives emigrated to Switzerland. She has been there many times and loves the way of life that the Swiss cherish so much. The shed is a small-scale reminder of lovely times spent in the Alps. The name 'Witt's End' was given by Grazia's husband, and has stuck ever since.

Grazia outside her shed

The walls are shiplap boards on the outside with timber panelling on the inside, all on a treated timber frame. The inside has been partly wallpapered and decorated. The shed has a complete electrical system of power points and switches – even though some need finishing!

Grazia's husband has a friend in the print business who managed to obtain some zinc printing plates to use as a roof covering. This works extremely well, though it is quite noisy when it rains. The inside of the roof has Rockwool insulation in order to help keep the heat in.

The timber shutters on the glazed windows are there purely to look good and add to the Swiss chalet style. One window facing the neighbours is obscured for privacy.

The stable door was made specifically from scrap wood. The various locks and handles have been salvaged from other doors or donated by friends.

Grazia is very proud of her little shed, even though she doesn't use it that much. Her friends and neighbours find it quaint and charming – like her, really!

BIKE SHED

When Bruce bought his house, it had a shed more or less where the present building is sited. The old shed was a rather overpowering, big, black corrugated building right outside the kitchen window. Something needed to be done about it, so Bruce began by building a kitchen extension which meant that the old shed was dismantled and re-erected further down the garden. A few years after that, Bruce was given a lean-to which was added to the end of the shed, making it twice as long. At the end of that he then built a potting shed, extending the building further again. He then found he needed even more space, so he took over the potting shed and built another one for that purpose. The whole building is now quite long, and his wife has said that 'there are to be no more sheds!'

Bruce has made the building very useful. Once inside it he can be really quite self-sufficient. He has installed solar panels which supply all of the shed's electrical needs, and there is a sink which is used for everything except washing up. A wood-burning stove (given to him as a gift) provides heat during the winter. Bruce is a real forager and is always looking for wood or other materials that other people throw away. He is also very creative and applies his creativity not only to solving practical problems for his work, or around the house, but also to decorative crafts. Bruce is careful about who comes into his shed. He would not take strangers in there, unless he trusted them. Friends, however, always find a warm welcome because Bruce is a warm-hearted, lovely, slightly eccentric individual.

Bruce in his shed

The walls are made of basic timber framing with feather-edge boards on the outside. Internally, there is so much material stacked against the walls that it acts as a kind of insulation. There was some fibre-board but that has deteriorated so much now that a new solution needs to be found. Externally, there are various creepers, which, according to Bruce, saves on painting with creosote. Plus, lots of small creatures inhabit the skin of the building, which he rather likes.

The corrugated roof panels have been mostly found and re-used. Some clear plastic panels had to be bought, and they let sufficient light into the building. There are various photo-voltaic panels sitting on the roof surface which provide basic electricity.

There are various windows on the shady side of the building, but not too many as most of the light comes from above.

The original floor was made of crazy paving, but that got a bit bumpy so Bruce dug it up and replaced it with a concrete base on which various floor coverings reside.

Bruce tries to obtain as much as possible by scavenging. For instance, when one of the roof beams was sagging, he managed to obtain an old piece of water pipe which he propped up under the beam. It is a quick, simple solution which will last decades, and at no cost whatever!

THE PONDEROSA

Tiggy's dad was nicknamed 'Tugger'. Somehow the name 'Tiggy' became the moniker for Michael (as he was christened). Now retired, Michael/Tiggy has been a lorry driver for the main part of his life. His allotment is a wonderful retreat in which he can potter around and grow vegetables. Tiggy shares the allotment and the shed with his good friend George. They both put in work and time, but George is fully employed so he can't spend as much time tilling the soil. The allotment sharing came about while George and Tiggy were drinking in their local; it seemed a good idea at the time to grow their own food. Within a couple of weeks an allotment plot was theirs.

As a driver, Tiggy used to deliver steel on large 8x4 ft pallets. He was able to obtain these large pieces of timber, with which the shed was constructed. The building came out not quite large enough, so George bought a small shed which was attached to the main building, like an annexe. Tiggy visits the shed almost every day: there's always something to be done. The only problem is occasional vandalism, broken windows mostly. George got fed up with this and put a notice on the shed door that read: 'IF YOU WISH TO USE THE SHED PLEASE DO SO, BUT DON'T SMASH THINGS UP', which seems to have had the desired effect.

The frame of the shed is made up of timber scavenged from various skips over the years. The outer skin is clad in something Tiggy calls 'Essex board' (a composite made up of slivers of softwood bonded with resin under high pressure). Some walls are made up entirely of glazed panels.

The roof is covered in several layers of roofing felt fixed with clout nails. Water is collected via PVC rainwater goods and stored in butts.

There are no defined windows as such. Whole areas of walls are glazed with scavenged windows and frames. Some are lozenge-leaded windows; some plain glass. Somehow the jigsaw of panels fits together with very few gaps. The effect inside is very light and airy – perfect for bringing on young plants.

The interior is very cosy. There is a gas cooker for preparing simple meals and brewing tea. An easy chair provides comfort when it's raining. Tiggy likes to sit there and read. The building has a warm, intimate feeling about it. It's very functional, and cost very little to build – the very essence of a shed.

The door is home-made from found materials. There is a padlock, but Tiggy says it's hardly worth locking because of the large amount of glass.

TWIN PEAKS

Tony built his shed some forty-five years ago. It was important to Tony that he built something 'in which he could do things'. He made the base using slabs. On top of bearers he put a substantial floor. This, of course, left a perfect void for rats and other vermin to move in. Tony had to lift some boards at a later date to get rid of the problem.

Being of an engineering disposition, Tony built the shed more or less as a cube so that the width and length were equal. He then measured the span for the roofing and ordered corrugated plastic sheets by post. These duly arrived, and it was only then that Tony realised he hadn't allowed for the slope of the roof: the sheets were exactly the same length as the span. That is why the shed has two pitches, one longer than the other.

Tony keeps all sorts of materials in his shed, including some bicycles with interesting modifications. He has had several occupations and is currently a sculptor working in metal. His garden and house make a domestic backdrop for the beautiful figures he makes, some of which are over three metres high. Unfortunately the shed, being of timber, is not suitable for welding purposes so he has had another lean-to built of blockwork on the side of the house.

The frame is made of timber with lapped boards for the exterior cladding. Some parts were painted with preservative, others with paint.

The shed has a twin-pitched, asymmetric roof. One part is covered in corrugated plastic sheets, the other in roofing felt.

The window is simply made and is sited over the work-bench, giving maximum light onto the surface.

The door was made using vertical and horizontal boards nailed together. It was made as a stable door, which would have meant that Tony could have worked in a draught-free shed. However, due to a lack of suitable bracing, the whole door has slipped on the fore-edge and the top half won't open. Also, as the door was very heavy; four extremely strong outrigger hinges had to be used in order to take the weight!

Tony likes to keep chickens, and they live next door in their own enclosure. The shed is a store, small workshop and bicycle garage. A yew tree was planted near one corner in order to give some shade, but Tony found that two small 'oiks' used the tree to climb onto the roof and jump about. Not one of his best ideas.

TEA CHALET

Kev works as a gardener for a lovely couple living in an old house. He calls the lady 'the boss' and her husband 'the guvnor' which helps when decisions are being made about what's to be done in the garden. The shed was built by a builder, so the whole building was made to fit into a particular space and for a specific purpose. It is a garden shed, and as such is used for storing tools, bringing on young seedlings, making repairs to tools, etc. It faces roughly south so it can get a bit hot in direct sun, but the view from the window is charming, looking out over vegetable beds and fruit trees. The shed was designed to look like an established building as it is sited very close to an old barn. Even though the shed is not much more than ten years old, it fits easily into the mix of old buildings and walls because of the sympathetic nature of its materials. The joke among friends and family is that 'Kev spends all of his time in the shed drinking tea' – hence the name Tea Chalet. Kev is very methodical and tidy. The shed has to 'be proper'. Everything is labelled and has its place.

The timber frame has feather-edge boards on the outside, while the inside is panelled. There is a lot of insulation between the studs in order to maximize energy conservation. The outside has been painted matte black.

The traditional slate roof is built in exactly the same way as in any well-built house and sits on tanalised timber battens, which are fixed to substantial rafters. The guttering collects and channels the rainwater into water butts.

There is a lot of mostly south-facing fenestration, which gives the interior an airy brightness.

The gardens are as orderly as the shed's interior.

A strong door is always a good idea for any shed, as it affords security against vandalism.

There is a proposal to put photo-voltaic panels on the roof which will provide enough electricity to power the lighting.

SEDUM SHED

Jan lives with her family in a delightful house with a modest garden at the rear. Since there was no room for a shed to be discreetly tucked away, it was decided to have one that would look attractive to the eye. The present building is a cross between a beach hut (Jan loves the sea) and a shepherd's hut (Jan's grandfather was a shepherd). A lot of research went into finding a maker who could create the shed of Jan's dreams. Luckily, one was found reasonably locally and the building commissioned. The roof deserves a special mention. The covering is of sedum, which is a living roof. It needs a little watering from time to time if the weather is dry but otherwise is more or less maintenance-free. In the later part of the year and into early spring, the plants have twiggy shoots. Jan rather likes the fact that birds use these for nest-building. The colour of the roof varies throughout the year and from side to side, the north face appearing slightly darker in shade. It was fascinating to watch the roof covering being 'laid' rather like a carpet or turf over the impermeable membrane on the roof. Jan is very proud of the shed and is pleased to show it to anyone who is interested. The shed is used for storage and for repairing bits and pieces.

Jan and her shed

The walls are of pine boards, painted on the outside and varnished on the inside, which gives the feeling of a Scandinavian building.

The top layer is of sedum, planted in a mesh which is then laid on top of a waterproof membrane. The shape of the roof is curved, like a railway carriage or shepherd's hut. This gives the interior structure a pleasing shape, with additional headroom in the middle.

The door is part-glazed, allowing additional light into the shed.

The windows are opening casements with fasteners and stays. In hot weather, the building is very well ventilated, which is real bonus as most sheds can get rather stuffy.

The main talking point is the curved, planted roof. Although such roofs have been used for centuries in places like Scotland (crofter's cottages use turf) it's unusual to find a planted roof in a domestic garden. Jan's neighbours love to gaze out of their bedroom windows at the colourful roof – a delightful change from roofing felt. Jan was a little worried about tree seedlings planting themselves on her roof and growing into mighty trees, but the roof is too dry for most plants.

WONDERLAND

Alice always wanted a shed for her allotment. She was very lucky to be offered a plot on a delightful site near her home. The allotments were given to the village by a charity in days gone by, specifically so that the village poor could grow their own food. The plots are very cheap to rent and are well used. Alice spends as much time as she can there and knows most of the people on the site. She wanted a small shed in which to store the usual tools, so she bought a very modestly-priced shed from a DIY chain. It took very little effort to put up. She keeps her bits and pieces in there and has often used the shed as a shelter from the rain. It's a little too far to walk home.

The wals are of overlapping boards on a simple, lightweight frame. The original colour was a horrible shade of orange. Very quickly after putting it up, Alice painted the shed 'a sensible colour'.

The roof is the usual felt. It has a simple gutter and downpipe which collect water into rainwater butts – very useful on the allotment.

A plain shed door offering the basic minimum.

The fenestration is very simple, just enough to allow light inside.

Alice has put up a small, bamboo flagpole which is now empty. The Union Jack is hanging inside the window as a sign of the patriotic fervour ignited during the 2012 Olympics.

JAMES SHED

Lee moved from London to his new home near the Chilterns with a big collection of motorabilia which needed a shed to live in. He didn't have time to have one purpose-made, so he had to buy one quickly and put it up in the garden. He soon realized that he needed more space, so Lee built himself an extension.

Lee has been collecting 'stuff' for over fifteen years. It began with the odd oil can, then came some interesting signs and mechanical objects such as padlocks. He always remembers collecting. First it was coins and stamps as they were easier to get hold of. Then came bigger things. Lee's father worked at Mulliner Park Ward, the Rolls Royce coachbuilders, and it was he who suggested that his son begin a career in the motor trade. Following an engineering apprenticeship, Lee worked in various small firms in London and developed his career as a specialist metalworker. He has always admired the craft and skills of days gone by; that's why he surrounds himself with beautiful hand-made objects. The only concession to the modern age in Lee's shed is electricity, with which he powers lights and a radio (and sometimes in winter a heater).

Lee gets most of his objects from auto jumbles; sometimes on eBay, and other specialist markets. Some of the tread plate names were donated by his father or friends. The lovely James motorcycle is taken out for an airing from time to time, just to keep it running. Lee observes: 'This little motorbike used to be the working man's bike in its day. I love it. It's small, compact and only 98cc!'

The walls are lapped boards, on a timber frame. There is dense insulation under the outer skin, and Lee has lined the interior walls and ceiling with T&G boards. These have been decorated and finished to the same high standard as his home.

The roof is covered in the usual roofing felt, with heavy insulation underneath. All the rainwater is collected via gutters and downpipes into two rainwater butts. A nice touch is that Lee has inserted a motor factor valve instead of the usual tap in one of the butts.

The door is double-skinned inside and out, with a braced frame internally. Special attention has been paid to good hinges and strong locks for security purposes.

The windows open but they face away from direct sun, as Lee didn't want sunlight causing paint to fade on signs and objects. There are only two windows as they allow a lot of heat to escape. And the inside wall space is precious.

The shed is like a mini-museum. Everything is clearly displayed on shelves. There is carpet on the floor and an air of quiet contemplation when you enter the building. It's a peaceful and interesting little building, and a great credit to its owner.

FERRET COURT

John bought a ready-made shed in which to house his ferrets, but soon found it to be too small. So he designed and constructed an 'extension' which he annexed to the original building. That too proved insufficient, so a separate, moveable little building was made and attached to the existing complex.

John's wife Jane originally said she wanted a pet, to which John said 'Why do you want a pet? You've got me!' To which she replied 'No, I want something small and furry!' So the quest was on to find a suitable candidate. Eventually they settled on a ferret. Some twenty years later, eight furry little ferrets live an enjoyable communal life, much loved and cherished by John and his wife. John has obtained these animals from various rescue centres and provided them all with a safe and interesting environment. He is most meticulous in keeping the sheds clean and well-maintained. He takes a lot of care of any animal that is unwell, taking it to the best veterinary practice and paying for any medicines required. John recalls one special ferret: 'He used to open the fridge in the kitchen. This became a bit irksome so I decided to buy a fridge which had a strong magnetic seal. It took the little devil three weeks to learn how to open the new fridge, but he got there!'

John makes beautiful walking sticks, and, of course, one of these has a ferret's head carved at its top. When he gets any spare time, John loves to take wildlife photographs and has built up a wonderful collection of images.

The walls of all the sheds are made of basic timber framing covered with shiplap boards, painted with preservative as necessary.

Like most sheds, the roof is covered in roofing felt. The rainwater is carried away using PVC guttering and downpipes.

Some windows are glazed, whilst the others are covered in strong mesh – ferrets can even gnaw away metal. In case the sun gets too strong, John has devised screens which can be used to shield the animals.

The main door is of the usual shed door construction. Various smaller doors have been made specifically to open in order to allow cleaning of the interior.

Apart from the custom-made shed complex, John has designed and made all of the runs and resting places inside the sheds. Some runs are made of spiral-wound gas flue; others of cloth or wood.

SHOOTER'S CABIN

John got his shed from Luton Airport some twenty years ago when work on the site was being wound down. The contractors didn't want the cabin so it was offered to John – they even delivered it for nothing! Not an easy task considering that the building sits at the edge of a field at the end of a long farm track. John has been running a shooting club for several decades, and he built his original trap house himself out of bits and pieces. The offer of a ready-made building was a god-send: at last the club members had somewhere to keep materials and brew up tea and coffee. All was rosy until John arrived at the shed one day to find that some vandals had set it on fire. Luckily the fire didn't get a hold, but it caused quite a bit of damage.

John began life wanting to be an agricultural engineer, but life has a habit of changing circumstances. By some family connection, John managed to join the armed forces, starting at the Army Apprentices School. During his time, John learnt to play the trumpet, and later was posted to Germany as a tank mechanic. Some time later John left the forces and opened a shop with his mother. As he knew a lot about firearms, he started the shooting club as a hobby and has run it ever since. All the members are friends, and John enjoys the 'craic' of shooting clays every fortnight or so.

The Portakabin has panel walls and is insulated. In addition, there are vertical metal studs which would allow the building to be stacked on another one.

The roof is made of plastic-coated aluminium panels which are corrugated. There is an overhang at the front which is useful when it rains. The fascia just under the roof is made of second-hand scaffold planks. There is a single pitch that drains into the field just behind the building. The ceiling inside was lined with board, but some damage has left the insulation dropping out.

There is a top-hung casement window at the front, which has good security when closed.

The door is a standard braced and boarded door.

There is nothing exceptional about the outside: it looks like many other Portakabins. But the shooting club members are very fond of the building which they call their home from home. John certainly treats it like his second kitchen.

MODELRAILWAYSHED

For around thirty years, Ken has lived with his wife in their 200-year-old cottage. When they first came to the house, the previous couple had been in the process of divorce proceedings and the man lived in an old caravan – Ken thinks it might be from the 1920s – in the garden, coming into the house only for evening meals. The wife lived in solitary splendour in the marital home. The owner's son had a real passion for model railways and had built one all around the inside of the timber shed. Anyone entering the shed had to duck under the trackway which ran across the door at waist height. When he left, he took his stuff with him and Ken spent some time making good and building a proper workbench.

Ken's grandchildren came round one day and went to play in the old caravan. They were about five or six years old and the adults, free from the chores of child-minding, were having tea and a lovely time in the house. After some time, someone said 'It's very quiet in the garden. I can't hear the kids at all.' So Grandad went down to the caravan and found the children in floods of tears. The door handle had dropped off on the inside and they couldn't get out.

The old caravan at the bottom of the garden.

The shed sits on brick piers. It has a timber floor and frame with the outside being clad with shiplap boards. The inside walls are lined.

The roof is of the usual roofing felt, having a single slope. The water is not collected, but just runs off into the garden.

Unusually for a small shed, the windows are Crittall metal framed ones. Such windows were used quite a lot in the post-war years, particularly in building council houses.

The door is a simple boarded type.

The 'NO SMOKING' sign on one of the shed's windows always draws comment. Ken thinks it came from London Transport, maybe a tube train. The outside of the building has some lovely pots and plants fixed to the wall, together with one or two ornaments. Plants creep along one wall which gives the shed a lived-in look; nature and building in harmony.

TRAILER VAN

To be precise, the shed which sits in the rear of Nicholas's car yard was originally built as a 'Steam Roller Driver's Living Van'. His father bought the trailer from a Dr Oliver Dancy. Actually, 'bought' is not quite right. The trailer was exchanged for half a dozen 750x16 Land Rover tyres, and no money changed hands. Dr Dancy had several old Land Rovers that needed new boots, while Nicholas's dad needed a shed, so it suited both men to do the deal. The trailer was towed to the family home where it stayed for some years. Then it was moved again to another home, finally resting up in the car yard. It has always functioned as a shed of sorts. For a while it was used by children as a play-room; later as an occasional office. For three years one of the mechanics lived in it in the corner of the yard (he came from Norfolk and didn't relish the 200-mile round trip every weekend). Nowadays the dogs use it and Nicholas and his son sometimes camp in it. The trailer was made in Rochester in around 1910 and follows the principles of wagon-building apart from the sub-frame and wheels, which are of metal more suited to a railway carriage.

Nicholas's son Jack

There is a window in each of the four faces of the trailer. These are of timber construction with opening casements.

There is a stable door which opens outwards. The top leaf has a rather elegant wrought-iron hook and eye to keep it open. Steps lead up to floor level.

The timber roof is curved, like many railway wagons, and covered in felt. The rainwater drains away to the ground. The felt has been replaced several times during the century or so of the trailer's lifespan.

The walls are clad with lapped boards over a timber frame. The inside is also lined, but there is no insulation.

The most obvious feature of the shed is that it looks like a wagon. The heavy metal sub-frame is engineered as if to withstand earthquakes! The metal wheels and solid tyres would have given the trailer a noisy, hard ride, but nothing compared to the steam roller that towed it. The cheerful colour scheme attracts many comments from visitors. How could anyone not love this little building?

THE OLD DAIRY

David's shed is attached to the main farmhouse hayloft or granary, where he has lived for the past forty years. It was originally a separate lean-to but was incorporated into the main roofline when the building was re-roofed. He thinks it might have been the dairy for the farm, since the walls are painted with limewash. It is thought that the shed may be between 150 and 200 years old, but it's difficult to determine as beams and timbers were often re-used from other buildings. David had been looking to move out into the countryside when, one day, a friend called to say that the farm granary and outbuildings were up for rent. He jumped at the chance and has been living there quite happily ever since. Now that he is retired, he spends his time riding, looking after his chickens, and going to various horse-related events. He hopes to have a Friesian horse of his own before long, having had two other horses previously.

The shed is used to store garden implements and the usual assortment of bits and pieces. David has some of his dad's saws and hammers hanging up. He does work in it sometimes, but the building is rather dark as it only has one window, and that's covered by ivy. The building is smothered in grasses and ferns almost as if it's part of the surrounding woodland. David loves all things natural and is very sympathetic towards plants, allowing them the freedom to grow as they like. Curiously, the floor slopes downwards away from ground level; a fact which has puzzled David for years.

Remnants of past lives hanging from an old beam.

The walls are of flint and brick construction held by lime mortar. The exterior is mostly brick (apart from the ivy) and the interior skin is mostly flint, all of which is limewashed. As is often the case with old walls, they are over 230 mm thick.

There is only one window, which has not been opened in years. In any case, ivy obscures most of the glass making the interior of the shed quite dark.

The roof timbers, from inside the shed, look very old and massively strong. The marks of carpenter's tools can be seen clearly on them. Most of the old timbers were made on site to suit their intended use. The steep pitch of the roof (steeper than most sheds) allows the building to appear larger than it actually is, due to the volume of interior space. The shed smells old: of paint, limewash, timber and so on. Therein lies its charm.

The slate roof sits on recently renewed battens and felt. Before that, the slates were hung on battens and boards, but the boards rotted away and these were replaced by felt. Using boards would make the roof quite rigid, and much easier to work on when putting it up. However, the felt makes the roof very watertight.

There is a timber, boarded door in a wooden frame. Although it's old, it has probably been replaced more than once, considering the age of the building.

THE WENDY HOUSE

There is no precise date for the construction of The Wendy House, which Peter owns. In one of the family albums there is an old photograph of the building being constructed. The shed was built in Buckinghamshire by Peter's grandfather who lived on a farm at the time. It would have been built for Peter's parents. They used it for playing in and having friends round for tea parties. At the time, the shed was painted very prettily and the name Wendy House stuck. After ten or twelve years, the grandparents sold the family farm and moved to Cumberland. Peter's father offered to give the shed a new home at his house in Hertfordshire. Since the shed had been built as bolt-together panels, it was a relatively easy job to take it to pieces and move it to its new location. A few years after that and following another local move, the shed was again dismantled and moved to its present resting place. Peter's father Geoffrey lined the walls with fibre-board and wallpapered the inside. A mezzanine platform was added with a rope ladder for access – it was very popular with boys! Later, when Peter was a teenager and interested in other things, The Wendy House ceased to be used as a play-room and became a storage shed for garden tools. The fibre lining attracted rats and birds so it had to be stripped off, back to the shiplap boards which form the present interior surface. Several repairs have been made over the years, but even after some seventy years the shed still looks very useful and will probably be inherited by Peter's son in due course.

The walls are of painted shiplap boards on a timber frame. The four wall panels were made on the ground on site and bolted together at the corners. The floor is boarded on a timber frame which sits on paving slabs.

The roof is of felt on top of boards. The roof trusses have been made specifically for this building by the craftsman who built the shed. There is no gutter so the rainwater just discharges to the ground.

There are four metal Crittall windows, which seem to have been second-hand when they were put in. Special frames were made to accommodate the windows and these were incorporated into the wall panels.

The plain timber door is made of vertical boards on a timber frame. Some repairs have been made, and several locks and handles have been used over the years.

Peter learns the art of mowing.

The shed was built as a play-room, but like many other sheds has changed its use as the needs of the family have evolved. Some birds have made their nests inside the roof space. Peter considers this to be good fortune.

MISSION CONTROL

Simon works in the motor industry. His shed is made from the segmented up-and-over shutter doors used in large garages. Some garage doors were being replaced, so Simon managed to get the old ones for nothing. Moving the large panels was a bit of a problem until Simon's brother-in-law stepped in with his van.

Simon's wife was 'intrigued' (Simon's word) when he arrived with all the panels in the van. While the old shed was being dismantled the garden was a bit full of 'stuff', but as the aluminium construction began to take shape she calmed down.

Having built his shed over one weekend, Simon stepped back into the garden in order to take a photograph to put up on Facebook. One of his friends noticed the furled-up washing line in the foreground of the picture and said 'It looks like a rocket with Mission Control in the background!' The name has stuck ever since. The aluminium segments of the old garage doors were quite easy to cut using a jigsaw, and the only elements Simon had to buy were a few brackets and plates so the sections could be joined together. The roof was made quite simply using boards and felt.

Simon is a keen angler. He keeps all his kit in the shed as it is too smelly to bring into the house. He is also very good at making things and has made some lovely cabinets for his home. The shed is very crowded but somehow there is just enough room for the small bench he uses.

Second-hand aluminium panels have been bolted together to make very strong walls. The whole building sits on a concrete base which was made before the building was put up.

The beauty of using an old garage shutter door for the walls is that it comes with its own integral windows! They don't open but the seals are very good against weather and burglars.

The door is made from the same aluminium sections as the walls. Simon has even re-used the hinges.

The simple, single-pitch roof is made of roofing felt nailed onto board. The water is collected and used for watering the garden. One small detail that Simon invented is his 'felt washer'. He has used roofing felt to effectively enlarge the area of the galvanized clout nail heads, thus giving a greater bearing surface than with a plain nail head.

The shed is very strong because of its metal construction. In winter the building can be a little cold and suffers a little from condensation, but Simon doesn't spend too much time there during the winter months.

THE GREEN SHED

According to Ron, who is very particular about the spelling of his family name, he is descended from a well-known Scottish king, Malcolm II. He was born in 1929 and almost died from mastoids when he was a child. Aged fourteen and wanting to see the world he joined the army. Ron was initially attached to the 10th Hussars Band at Borough Castle before joining another regimental band at Arborfield, along with three other boys. He had always wanted to play the drums. He only recently found out that his father had also played percussion in the army during the First World War. Although Ron asked to play the drums, he was initially given the job of playing the cornet. He was lucky enough to be put under the charge of a Band Sergeant who was one of the best drummers in the Army. So Ron had a marvellous teacher, and history repeated itself. Ron recalls 'My teacher was a bit hard – they were in those days – sometimes when I went wrong he used to throw his boot at me. At other times, he'd stand behind me and hit me over the head with a drumstick when I made a mistake!' The first ever public performance of Ron playing drums (with a seven-piece band) was at a posh dance at Farley Castle where the music went down pretty well.

After his Army years, Ron joined a band (one of many throughout his career), got married and had a family, although not necessarily in that order! He has had many occupations during his life: musician, gardener, teacher, salesman and so on, but music has always been his main passion. Even now he plays percussion in his shed most days. He is also a gourmet. He bakes his own bread and grows his own vegetables in a delightful garden around his home. The Green Shed is small, but unique amongst sheds as a rehearsal room.

The walls are shiplap boards, painted on the outside, fixed to a simple wooden frame. Ron has planted vines and flowers around the shed in order to soften the hard lines of the building.

The roof is made of felt over board. The shed is made of three parts: the music section plus two others which house logs and garden equipment. All of them are joined together.

There is some glazing but it does not open; it is only there to allow light into the interior.

This is of the simplest braced frame construction. There is a good, strong lock on it so that Ron's precious artefacts are well protected.

Although most of the shed complex is used for log storage and garden bits and pieces, its most important function is to make music. Along with cymbals, memorabilia and other stuff, Ron is very proud of his Vibraphone, which is a beautiful instrument looking like a xylophone with sewing machine parts added. The sound it produces is haunting and lovely.

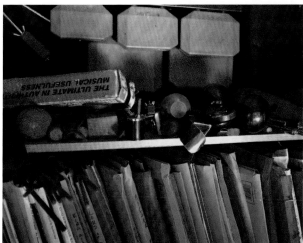

THE GLASS SHED

Ever since she was a small girl, Michelle has had a fascination for cleaning glass panes and mirrors. Originally from Essex, she only recently moved to her present house. One of its most attractive characteristics was that it had a ready-made glass 'shed' – as Michelle calls it. To most people it looks like a conservatory, but Michelle was thrilled by the huge expanse of glass which would allow her plenty of light and give her passion for glass an outlet. She uses the shed in much the same way as many other people would: somewhere to store bits and pieces, where she can read or do some sewing, pursue her hobbies, or plant out pots for the garden. During the summer months Michelle gets annoyed by flies. 'All these flies keep coming in and crapping on the glass, so it needs constant cleaning. I clean it most days.'

One of Michelle's great pleasures is sitting in her shed admiring the view and her garden. She is very fond of nature and likes to sit inside while it's raining outside. She loves the sound and sight of rain, and being able to see everything all around.

The walls, as such, are fully glazed. The frame is all aluminium, bolted at the corners. It's a thin-gauge material which makes it light and strong. The whole building sits raised up on a timber platform which rests on timber joists and concrete piers.

The roof is also fully glazed. It is of a single pitch and attached to the main house. There is a moulded aluminium gutter which discharges into a narrow-diameter plastic downpipe.

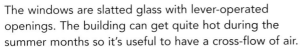

The windows are slatted glass with lever-operated openings. The building can get quite hot during the summer months so it's useful to have a cross-flow of air.

There are two sliding doors, again of aluminium and glass. These are lockable on the inside in much the same way as a greenhouse or conservatory.

Michelle is very proud of her little glass shed, and rightly so. She keeps it clean and tidy – she doesn't like a mess – and, although it's quite small, she loves it. She cannot imagine being without it.

THE LOVE SHACK

Winnie and her husband Joe wanted a 'bolt hole' – somewhere they could escape from the hurly-burly of a big city. They had no particular place in mind, but thought Brighton might be nice. Some friends introduced them to this lovely location by the sea and it was love at first sight. A factory-made shed was bought and put up some twenty or so years ago. Winnie and Joe stay in the shed as often as possible. They entertain friends and have shed parties; and a local dog called Baxter has adopted them. The shed is often left empty and vandals have occasionally broken the windows. Once, they even tried to set fire to it. But that doesn't deter Winnie: she's tough, and gets on with life. Their neighbours are kind and friendly. All of them seem to come to the seaside seeking peace and tranquility and an escape to a slower world. Most of the shed is furnished with stuff donated or found. Winnie has decorated the cupboards using animal-print fabric, which almost makes them into art objects. If the furniture was in a bijou shop in London it would fetch a good price and be highly collectable.

The walls of the shed are made of shiplap boards, fixed horizontally upon a timber frame. The whole building sits on a platform made of timber decking, which is fixed to a frame. Timber upright 'piles' are sunk 1.5 m into the ground, and the deck is about 1.2 m above ground level.

The shed has a felt roof on boards; it has had to be replaced as the original felt deteriorated.

There were two windows, one on each side, but due to vandals breaking them, they have been boarded up.

A pair of half-glazed doors allows light to come into the building, particularly in the afternoons.

The interior is very welcoming. Delightful objects can be found all over the walls and ceiling. Of course, the space is a bit small, but it's surprising how the shed has most of the creature comforts needed for a simple life. Colourful fabrics are everywhere. Winnie is the queen of her castle by the sea.

THE BLOCKER'S RETREAT

The Blocker's Retreat was built in 2007, and so named because there was a pub next door called The Blocker's Arms (there used to be a lot of straw-plaiting done locally for the hat trade). Anne lives in a small house with a small garden. There was a shed on the present site but it didn't use the space effectively, so it was decided to make a custom-built shed which would utilize as much of the space as possible. A local craftsman was employed. In order to fit it into the corner near the wall, the frame was built and two sides clad in feather-edge board before the entire building was pushed right into the corner using metal rollers and the rest then finished off.

The shed has many uses. Anne stores her bikes in it. During hot summer months she sleeps in it and allows her visitors to do this. She reads in it and sometimes has meals there. If it's raining, she does occasional DIY in it. Anne is a wine connoisseur, and her next plan is to consider digging a big pit under the floor to make into a wine cellar – she is thinking of a capacity of one thousand bottles.

The building has wattle-and-daub front walls – the interior and wattle can be seen by lifting a panel inside. Anne enjoyed doing the wattling with her builder. The side and back walls are of 150 mm featheredge boards. The whole frame is of 100x75 mm tanalised timbers. The interior is partly panelled and partly plastered in order to try to give the building an aged look.

There is a lead roof (Anne wanted a permanent solution rather than the usual felt) upon 150 mm T&G boards. The ceiling has been lined with polystyrene in order to conserve heat. The whole roof sits on timber trusses which are quite substantial in order to take the weight of the lead roof.

The door was purpose-made as a stable door so that Anne could keep the draught out while enjoying fresh air. A small glazed window brightens up the upper half of the door. A particular detail is the door handle which is made from a yew branch and some galvanised wire. Everyone who sees it is fascinated by it.

There are two windows, one on either side of the door, plus a Velux window in the ceiling allowing plenty of light into the interior.

There are other unique elements as well as the quirky door handle. On the back wall, scratched into the plaster, is Anne's coat-of-arms and the date of construction. Every visitor loves the wattle and daub, in particular its little cover on which is written 'Secret revealed: Oak, Hazel, Straw, Sand, Lime, Wattle, Daub & Patience.'

LOO SHED

When Guy first came to his present house some thirty years ago the garden was a wilderness. At the bottom of the jungle there were two small buildings joined together; one was an outside toilet and the other a ramshackle store. As Guy began to clear the debris, he found that the toilet had long since stopped working so he dismantled it and gave the bowl (which was dated about 1820) to the local museum. For nostalgia's sake he kept the front of the cast iron cistern and its chain; both items now hang on the wall as a reminder of past glory. The original building would have had a slate roof, like the house, but that had collapsed long ago, so Guy replaced the roof with clear plastic sheeting: this lets in light and keeps out the weather.

Some time after doing up the loo shed, Guy added another extension to form an L-shape. This serves as a small greenhouse for growing tomatoes, cucumber and the like. Some of the tendrils of the greenhouse find their way into the shed, but Guy allows nature to take its course – as long as it doesn't take over!

The original roof would have been slate on top of battens. As that had collapsed, it was replaced by clear, corrugated PVC sheeting. This is both strong and light, as well as allowing plenty of natural daylight into the interior (and the occasional plant). The shed has no windows as the main source of light is from its roof. The PVC gutter discharges into a plastic water butt.

The door is made of timber. Its planks have a beaded edge which make the joints rather elegant. On the back of the door, three horizontal rails hold everything together. The hinges and latch are quite old and it makes a lovely change from the usual mass-produced tee-hinges available from most 'DIY sheds'.

Guy is very fond of history, and has gone to some pains in order to keep some original features, such as the lime plaster. Patches of this can be seen on the garden wall side of the shed. The cistern and chain are further reminders.

THE BULL PEN

Bob lives in an elegant timber-framed building surrounded by open country. In the farmyard attached to the main house are several barns and sheds. One of these is a small brick-and-slate shed used to house the pony and trap – half for storing the vehicle, the other half a small stable for the horse. This was Bob's shed until his son Tom had designs on it. As a consequence, all of the garden implements, tools and other jumble usually found in sheds had to be moved. The shed known as the 'bull pen' seemed a perfect alternative for Bob to move into. Although the front of the new shed is open to the weather, most of it is kept out by the large overhang and the corrugated panel on the gate. In winter it gets very cold, but in summer the building feels light and airy. Bob thinks the bull pen was built in the mid 1930s, but it's difficult to be certain. Like many buildings in a farmyard, the original opening would have faced the main barn and yard. However, the opening was changed to face away from the yard at a later date. This was done because, as Bob explains 'With stock, it's better for the animals to face the sun. If the building was used to store carts then it wouldn't matter.'

There are no windows in the walls but the roof does have one or two clear PVC corrugated panels which allow light in. The shed has electricity to provide for lighting and the use of power tools.

The walls are a combination of 230 mm local brick and a timber frame made of studwork with overlapping planks on the side opposite the doorway. Some of the internal walls have been lined with horizontal planks so that Bob can hang tools on the surface. This also stops draughts coming through.

The door is in fact a gate, typical of many farmyards. The bars are covered by a sheet of corrugated iron which has been painted green to match the garden.

The smell of timber, dust and old oils is the first impression gained on entering. Birds have made nests in the eaves. Dozens of horseshoes adorn the main tie-beam. Rosettes from many horse shows brighten the drab, untreated wood. Bob and his wife recently celebrated their fiftieth wedding anniversary and the hanging baskets from that event have become permanent displays at the front of the shed, adding a lighter touch to a purposeful building.

THE COW SHED

The odd nomenclature of this shed came about almost by accident. Chris's friend, Peter, had a son who was helping with the building work; the boy found a toy cow and said 'Can this be in it?'. So without hesitation, the toy cow was screwed to one of the uprights there and then, and it's been called 'the cow shed' ever since. The story guarantees to bring a smile to everyone who hears it. Chris wanted a refuge in which he could train without having to fork out the high cost of a gym membership, so he set about making his shed at the bottom of the garden. Most of it has been made from fencing panels and odds and bits. The only items he had to buy were the corrugated roof panels, plus screws and hinges. His wife and children also use the facilities, especially during the winter months when it's too bad to train outside. Chris maintains 'I have offered the use of the shed and its facilities to various friends, but they take one look at it and usually decline!'

The shed has its own disco, of sorts. Chris had an old amplifier which has been rigged up with speakers so that music can be played. Because of this, several parties have been successfully held in the shed, which, due to its position well away from neighbours, have largely gone unnoticed.

The roof is made from large sheets of industrial, square, corrugated aluminium panels. These are fixed to a simple frame. The surface of the metal is plastic-coated so needs no maintenance.

There is only one window, which is of plastic PVC sheet. This is screwed to a timber frame.

The door, or doors (in two halves) are made from one large fence panel. To counteract the enormous weight and leverage, Chris has had to use several tee-hinges to hold the lower door. A separate, wedge-shaped leaf closes the upper opening.

The shed sits on steeply sloping ground, so the base had to be built up to a level point with ready-mix concrete. Once a horizontal platform was made, the floor was put down using plywood panels.

One of the shed's best features is its position and outlook. Set away from housing, it is invisible from the main house. When inside the shed, the view from the window is one of rolling farmland looking northwards. The construction is mostly of fence panels, so the building is fairly unpretentious and modest. It doesn't shout its presence.

SMALLHOLDER'S SHED

This shed, which is completely smothered in creepers and flowering plants, is made from reclaimed materials. All of the timbers, tiles and other items are all second-hand. Elizabeth and her husband had scavenged among demolition yards, skips and rubbish dumps in order to obtain enough material with which to build a shed. It was, in fact, a lean-to, in that it was built alongside a bigger workshop building. For most of the time, the door stays open; it is well shrouded in hanging plants in any case, and when it rains, water never manages to find its way into the building. Like most sheds, it is used as a store for recycling materials, old bikes, long forgotten things in plastic bags and so on. Most visitors have never even seen a shed like this and are intrigued by the dark entrance, finding themselves drawn into the gloomy interior. Dogs and chickens take refuge in it at night, and children find it all magical.

The timber-framed walls are clad in lap boards, all of which are reclaimed. Foliage hides most of the walls and windows, thus making the interior very dark.

The old windows have not been opened for years. The creepers outside prevent any light wanting to penetrate the interior.

The door is made up of a timber frame, onto which is fixed an old estate agents' sign, which, being made of plywood, keeps the door frame square.

Undoubtedly the most obvious feature is the fact that the building is completely hidden from view. Normally, Elisabeth would keep the greenery cut back, but this year 'it's got away a bit'.

Second-hand pantiles cover the roof. The rafters and battens are all re-used from other buildings long gone. In one corner of the roof, a beautiful twisted brick chimney escapes from the mass of greenery.

THE WINE SHED

The solid building at the end of Giuseppina's garden is purpose-made for winemaking, and was built over twenty years ago by a family friend. The shed which first occupied the site had been built on a concrete base, but that was not adequate for the Wine Shed; so proper, one-metre-deep footings were dug and the new shed built upon those. The blockwork walls have been pebble-dashed, so that the shed should last as long as the house.

Giuseppina came to the UK from Italy some half a century ago. Like many Italians of that time, she longed for the food and drink of her own country, which was difficult to find locally. Around the month of October, which is the winemaking season, Italians would converge from all over the south-east of Britain to the London fruit markets. There they would buy boxes of grapes (Montepulciano being a favourite) and take them back to their sheds in order to make wine for the family. This is exactly what Giuseppina and her husband Antonio used to do. Sometimes the wine press was shared among several families, being passed around for pressing the grapes. But each family had its own shed for storing the wine, which ran into several hundred litres per year.

According to Giuseppina, 'The men were good at doing all the heavy work, but they were too casual about cleanliness. It was the women who made sure that the carboys and demijohns were scrupulously clean, otherwise the wine would go sour.'

The walls of this shed are built of concrete blocks which are pebble-dashed externally. The concrete base is solid enough to take a three-storey building, let alone a shed. Internally, the blocks are left unpainted; it's better to have a dark interior for the wine.

There is one window opposite the main door, but this is partially blocked from the inside in order to restrict light coming into the shed. A dark interior is good for keeping wine and oil.

The only door into the shed is a solid one, painted brown. Sometimes, during very hot days or nights, this is left ajar to allow some air to circulate within.

Although the roof was originally of composite board on rafters with felt on top, an added layer of protection has been fixed over the felt. Bituminous, corrugated sheets have been added in order to guarantee absolute waterproofness.

Giuseppina did not make wine last year because she still has about 350 litres of white and red wine to get through. Her children have grown up and married so the wine is only brought out at family gatherings: she drinks very little on her own. Her eldest son likes to get involved in winemaking, but he has a busy family life so it's difficult to find the time.

GUITAR SHED

Paul moved to his present house about four years ago. He had begun making guitars whilst living in his previous house, where he had a shed. Because the new house didn't have a shed, Paul was working on his guitars on a bench in the garden. This situation could not go on for long, so Paul decided that he must have a shed. First, he had to go through the planning process with his wife, but once she'd given the approval he bought a building which was erected at the foot of the garden.

Paul commutes into London every day, so his time is very limited. Nevertheless, he wanted to take up a hobby that involved making something with his hands. He decided to build guitars even though he is not particularly musical. Crafts have always been in Paul's family; one of his grandfathers had been a stonemason, and the other a cabinet maker (in fact, some of the furniture made by his granddad is still in the family). So it was inevitable that the creative genes would manifest themselves one day. Paul has never learned formally how to make guitars: 'I knew that I wanted to make guitars, so I just bought a book, studied it avidly and made mistakes as I went along.' He doesn't sell the guitars or even play them much; he just wants to become really good at making something well, so that perhaps one day he can pass the skill and the instruments down to his children.

The original shed is made of lapped boards on a timber frame. Since building the first shed, Paul has had to add an extension which gives him a bit more space. He hadn't realized just how much room power tools take up.

Paul's workbench faces the windows which run the entire length of one wall and allow in enough light during daylight hours. However, some additional lighting is necessary for the intricate work necessary to build a musical instrument.

The timber door on the old building will be moved to fit into the new extension before winter comes. It is important to have good security, as some of the timbers and veneers used in guitar building are worth hundreds of pounds.

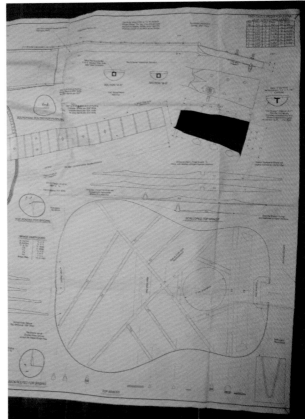

There are no distinctive features about Paul's shed, and he likes it that way. He prefers to have an anonymous building at the bottom of the garden. He has painted it brown, so that it looks very much like any other shed in the country. But it's the craftsmanship within that makes Paul's shed special.

MODEL RAILWAY SHED

Richard describes himself as a die-hard model railway enthusiast. His ambition was to have a large model railway layout, so the only solution was to buy a shed and build the project. His shed came from a manufacturer in Buckinghamshire and, once it was built a dozen or so years ago, Richard proceeded to design his layout. The whole layout took about five years to construct and is based on a town in France where Richard used to go on holiday. The model-making is of superb quality: tiny boats and their fishermen float upon little flowing rivers; sunbathers lie on the grassy banks (some topless as it's France!); lamp-posts on platforms light up at night, and so do all the tiny buildings; all the signals work. The whole layout looks very impressive in the dark. Richard has the utmost patience and skill. Everything is thoroughly researched and then accurately made. Even on holiday, he takes some model-making with him in case of rainy days.

Richard's attention to detail is illustrated by the story of the viaduct, part of his railway layout. He'd seen pictures of the structure in a book and even managed to obtain some plans. Even so, he wanted to actually visit Brittany and photograph it for himself but, as he adds, 'I managed to get there and found nothing at all. Very unreasonably, the French Army had blown up the redundant viaduct as part of a training exercise. So I had to go by the plans.' When Richard retires he would like to take an active part in operating one of the heritage railway lines, maybe by being a level-crossing operator or something similar.

The roof is of the usual roofing felt which is fixed to tongue and grooved boards.

The door is a braced and boarded tongue-and-groove construction. Some railway memorabilia decorates the outside, giving a small clue as to what lies within.

The shed walls are simple lapped boards on a timber frame. Preservative is regularly applied to the outside in order to keep the weather out.

The windows are of wooden construction with some opening casements.

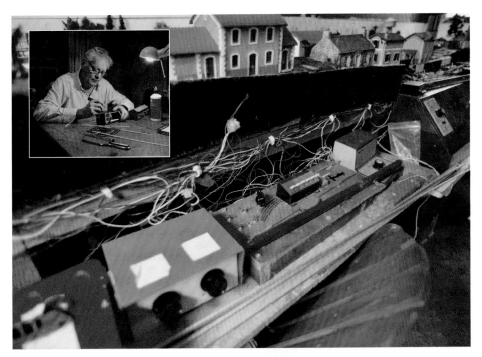

The main feature of this building is the miniature world of railway magic which has been constructed out of one passionate man's imagination and skill. Everyone, old or young, who visits and sees the layout is enchanted by it. A few damp winters and some condensation have caused one or two minor problems, but Richard is even now thinking about his next layout in a new building.

DANIELMANIA SHED

Mike has lived in his present house for several years; the house dates back to the mid-1920s. As far as he knows, the building he calls his shed – originally built as a garage – has never housed a car but has always been used as a shed.

Mike has spent a lifetime working as a journalist. He began at the very bottom as an office boy, then junior reporter and gradually rose to be a sub-editor, then an editor and finally group editor for a newspaper group. There is a large filing cabinet in the shed which houses many magazines and articles. His wife Jean is very organized and keeps track of all the filing and other mementoes. Mike was the author of a small book about cycling and time trials, called *5-4-3-2-1* as well as writing articles for *Sporting Cyclist* and *International Cyclist*.

Mike's shed is very solidly built of brick and the interior stays surprisingly dry. As he says 'Oddly enough, the shed is always dry. There's no heating in there and if I had found a problem with condensation I would have brought the magazines and articles back into the house. Winter and summer the temperature is fairly constant. It's extraordinary; it's very, very dry.'

The building is very solid; the walls are of 230 mm brick construction, with a proper damp course and concrete foundations. The shed is contemporary with the main house and follows similar design cues.

The timber-framed windows are original and have opening casements.

Clay pegtiles make up the roof, which has four hips and a beautiful line of red ridge tiles along the top edge. Under the tiling, the construction is of timber rafters and ceiling joists, with a plaster ceiling inside the shed. A fascia all around holds the guttering which was originally of cast iron, but has been more recently replaced by PVC. A downpipe and butt collects the rainwater.

The timber half-glazed door is placed opposite what would have been the garage door (which has been kept as a large opening in order to make access to the shed very easy).

There is nothing particularly outstanding about the building, apart from the fact that it sits perfectly in its environment. The materials used for the bricks and the tiles were made from local clay and fired nearby. It was constructed at a time when craftsmen worked on site rather than in a remote factory. The design is very conservative and pays respect to local building tradition and the vernacular. It may only be a shed, but it's a happy building.

WHEELWRIGHT'S SHED

According to Aubrey, the original building was constructed in the late 1890s, as a wheelwright's shed. When Aubrey arrived on the scene, some forty years ago, the shed still had a wonderful pyramid brick flue and forge in the middle of it. Following a long period as a wheelwright's shed, it was then turned over to the manufacture of bicycles and later motor-bikes, culminating in the building's present use in the restoration of classic cars. The basic construction has remained original in that the shed has a timber frame under a slate roof. Many additions and extensions have been added to the shed reflecting its varied use over the generations.

Aubrey's own background is in heavy engineering. He served his apprenticeship as a fitter/millwright and worked in industry for a period, ending up as the Chief Engineer in a chocolate production company. Aubrey recalls 'We had some impressive machines. I worked with some big spanners! We had a lathe with a 14 ft chuck, and it was 38 ft long!' Following a change in circumstances, he decided to concentrate on working with cars. He had always loved the Jaguar XK120 as a boy and one day had the opportunity to buy six of them, which he did. Many years later, Aubrey still has one of those XK120s: 'I drove it home for £75! In fact, it's still under restoration even now.'

The Victorian timber frame is still the original structure. The outside is mostly clad in feather-edge boards, but some parts of the outer walls have had lean-tos added, so the exterior is a hotch-potch of different materials that hide the original building.

The clay tile roof has nibbed tiles sitting on battens. The underside of the tiles and battens are still visible from inside.

The fenestration is varied, to say the least. Some light comes in from above, via translucent panels set in the roof; some through windows and frames made in situ to suit the building, There are very few opening lights so not much heat is lost.

The building has several doors, some small and some large. This is necessary in order to allow vehicles to be brought in and out of the space.

On entering, you are greeted by the sound of metal being worked. Old machines with wonderful names like 'The Ranalah' litter the space, no doubt used by generations of fitters and engineers and still going strong. Patterns for unusual cars adorn the walls. Faded photographs and newspaper cuttings of scantily-clad women jostle for wall space with unusual tools. The interior is a hive of industry where trained craftsmen turn out amazing sculptures in metal destined for a full classic car restoration. Thank goodness for such places.

BOATSHED

The ex-Beatle George Harrison donated this shed and Manor House, with its surrounding land, to the Hare Krishna movement some two decades ago. At that time the shed was in a very poor condition, but gradually it was renovated and now serves as the gardener's shed. The site has a theological college, a small school, some formal gardens, a productive garden and a dairy farm with working oxen. Fruit and vegetables grown here are used on the estate, with any surplus being sold. One of the little known activities of the movement is called 'Food for all' which does a remarkable thing: every day, 800 delicious and nutritious hot meals are cooked and taken out into London where the food is given out free to students and the homeless.

The incumbents at the Manor see themselves as custodians of the land, and, as such, they do not use pesticides or herbicides on the soil, preferring to use natural methods instead. Oxen are used to cultivate the land or move materials. There is another shed on the site called the Volunteer Shed. This building hosts various volunteer groups who come and work in harmony with the land under supervision, as at times like harvest, a lot of extra manpower is always required.

The pace of life is in tune with the working speed of animals and the seasons and weather; it all produces a tranquil and peaceful environment. This is evident when one sees Uddhava, the Gardens Co-Ordinator, quietly reading his gardening magazine in front of the shed.

The structure is of timber frame, with lapped boards on the outside. The interior has been lined with plywood which provides a strong, box-like rigidity.

There is one single door from the landward side and a double door on the lakeside. Both doors are timber framed and lapped boards on the outside.

The roof is covered in clay pegtiles hanging on roof battens. Under the battens the ceiling is tongue-and-groove boards. Purlins sit on two large trusses with steel tie-rods connecting the walls.

There is only one fixed window above the doors, looking out over the lake. This is the only form of natural daylight getting into the building, apart from when the doors are

The building is contemporary with the Manor House and shares some of the same design features, such as the decorated barge-boards. Since the building was built, the surrounding trees have grown quite large and provide welcome shade during hot summers: very useful in a shed with no opening windows! Around the walls and on the ceiling people have written their names or short messages; an age-old ritual practiced all over the world.

MUSIC SHED

The main shed is divided into two: Nicky's part of the shed is where she teaches languages and music, and the other part is used for storage. Nicky's family is very much involved in music and there are instruments and libretti and opera scores all over the place. She's very pleased to have her father's music in her shed, so she is very much at home in the building. She has a little garden plot directly in front of the shed which gives her great pleasure when the sun shines: it's wonderful to see stuff growing.

'Once I'm out there in the shed,' notes Nicky 'I am in another world. I lose all track of time. I can practice my singing, or translate, without being disturbed, no matter what's going on in the main house.' The shed was bought from a shed manufacturer and when it arrived, Nicky was delighted to see that the interior lining is of cedar; it always smells wonderful, especially after a damp night.

At present, Nicky's two adult sons also store bikes and other belongings in her shed, but she's hoping that, when they eventually settle down, she will have the shed to herself. She is very liberal about other people using her shed or her desk. 'I really don't mind if another member of the family wants to use the shed for anything; as long as they don't gum the whole place up!'

The shed has a factory-made timber frame, clad on the outside with cedar shiplap boards. The interior is clad a similar material, which gives great rigidity to the structure.

As is often the case, the roof is covered with that ubiquitous of all shed coverings: roofing felt. There are no gutters, so that the rainwater is not collected.

There are opening timber-framed windows on two walls.

The half-glazed timber door allows additional light into the shed.

The shed is many things for Nicky. It is part museum, having some of her father's souvenirs and mementoes of people the family have met or productions that have been staged. It is a practice room where songs can be sung without disturbing neighbours and it is a library for books about music. It acts as a small store-room for interlopers' belongings: unfinished jig-saw puzzles litter a surface awaiting completion. Onions hang from a nail in the sun. The smells of these mix with cedar wood and chain-oil from the bikes, creating an olfactory delight.

THE PAINTING SHED

Peter is an artist and always wanted his own shed to use as a studio. He didn't want a draughty, poorly-built shed, so he went for an oak-framed building. The Painting Shed is a beautifully made, traditional post-and-brace structure, using English oak. It is also well insulated and warm, as painting involves a lot of time spent standing up.

Peter's old cottage and garden has a high viewpoint overlooking rolling fields and distant hills. The shed, therefore, had to fit in with the vernacular architecture. It also had to have a lot of glazing so that the views could be enjoyed, so he decided to have a lot of window area both from a southerly aspect and via Velux windows in the roof. The number of windows, together with the gallery-like white walls, make the interior very light and airy. Most evenings, as the sun begins to set, pheasants and other creatures wander into Peter's garden, completely oblivious to the artist behind the glass. He has never enjoyed painting so much as he does in this shed. Sometimes, he paints all day without realising the time; until he is summoned for supper.

The oak frame was supplied and put up by a specialist firm. The outside is clad in feather-edge boards and painted black, to suit the local style. Inside the walls, dense insulation retains the heat in winter and allows the shed to stay relatively cool in summer. The inside walls are lined with plasterboard, skimmed in plaster and painted white.

A slate roof keeps the rain out. The slates are fixed onto tanalised battens, on roofing felt. The oak frame is post and brace with purlins supporting the rafters. The interior is heavily insulated with Rockwool.

All windows are double-glazed in timber frames. Some are opening casements, which, together with the doors, allow plenty of air to circulate when open.

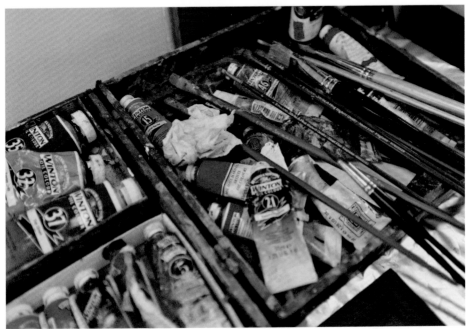

Undoubtedly one of the finest aspects of this little building is the commanding position on a hill overlooking open countryside. Peter has gone to great lengths in order to make the building fit into its context. The style of building, together with the colours used, all contribute to the fact that the shed looks very comfortable on its site. Once the years have passed and the woodwork has become a little weather-worn, there is no doubt that this beautiful, sturdy painting shed will look as if it was always meant to be here, cosy and settled by the parent cottage.

JAN'S SHED

'I am known as Wocko, throughout the country, and throughout the world. I even met some people in Australia a few years ago. They said, "oh you're Wocko aren't you?" So I am Wocko to everyone.' So says the builder of this wonderful shed, which he made for his wife Jan. She makes hats, baskets and other hand-made woven objects using natural fibres, rush, willow, sometimes even gladioli leaves, and so on. The smell pervading the entire building is one of oak, twines, leaves and other more unusual odours of the soil. As Wocko puts it 'It's mainly the bundles of rush, cut from the Ouze, which smell the most strongly. You go in the shed, in winter, you close your eyes, and it smells of summer. On a miserable day you go in there and the scent pervades your nostrils and it immediately evokes sunshine and long, lazy days.'

Many years ago, when Wocko and Jan first moved to their cottage, there was a garden shed already there. It had small windows with glass panes which gradually fell out and were never replaced, as Wocko is not good with glass: wood is his thing. Eventually the poor building fell to pieces, so it was replaced with the present shed. Wocko has been a woodsman all of his life, so the building had to be of timber construction. It took some time to build, and still needs a bit of finishing, but Jan finds it spacious and airy, and a delight in which to create her work.

The walls are of oak-frame construction, the wood coming from the nearby woods. The whole building sits on dwarf walls which have brick quoins with rubble and flint infill. The floor is a solid concrete raft sitting on a hardcore base. Externally, and lower down, the cladding is of waste sheets of plywood found thrown away. Some parts of the upper walls are clad in oak shingles or corrugated metal sheets.

The roof trusses are mostly made from damaged oak gateposts, sawn up to make smaller joists and beams. The roof aspect facing the cottage is covered with oak shingles, each one hand-cut by Wocko, and some being rounded for decorative effect. The north side of the roof is of corrugated iron sheets, awaiting replacement by more shingles.

All of the window frames have been made from oak. The windows face south so that Jan can have maximum light onto her bench and also enjoy a lovely view of the garden.

The glazed door is second-hand – someone was throwing it away. It affords a little extra light into the building.

Over recent years, Wocko has cleft out some 32-inch boards which will be used to feather-edge some of the walls, but it hasn't happened yet. Meanwhile, the shed has settled nicely into its woodland setting; a perfect end to the garden.

FUSING GLASS SHED

The Fusing Glass shed was found abandoned and then dismantled and brought to its present site. Tessa was a painter originally, and worked in the loft of the house. However, as soon as she began working with glass, it proved to be very difficult carrying materials up and down stairs, so the shed was a necessity. Once the kiln was installed in the original shed, there was not enough room, so it had to be extended to make extra space. Once Tessa started becoming known as a stained glass artist, her work began to get bigger so the shed had to be extended yet again. This time the shed extension came from a friend in London who was disposing of her shed.

Eventually the shed had to be extended yet again when Tessa was commissioned to make some rather large church windows. Somehow, there never seems to be enough space, no matter how big the shed may be. Every corner and surface is covered by sketches, ideas, pieces of glass and so on: works in progress. The bench that is used as a layout space was found abandoned by the side of the road. It is an old carpenter's bench, the signs of the woodwork vice being still visible at one side. It's a perfect working height, and even has tool wells at each end.

The walls are clad in vertical sheets of corrugated iron. This is a little cold in winter, but the inside is lined with flat sheets and insulation. Besides that, the kiln, when it's on, provides a lot of added heat.

The roof is a single pitch covered by corrugated iron sheets.

Light is Tessa's stock in trade, so there are a lot of windows, mostly east and south facing. The glass panes are adorned with little panels of coloured glass everywhere.

The door, unusually, is of corrugated iron on a wooden frame.

This small, metal building sits oddly in a woodland setting. It evokes a pre-war time when many agricultural buildings were built using corrugated iron sheets. When asbestos became commonly used, it replaced iron as the material of choice in farm buildings. However, as the shed has been in the garden for so long, it has weathered well and seems to have adopted its environment; a functional and unpretentious little shed.

THE CARVERY

All the materials for Tim's shed came from a nearby skip-hire business and cost virtually nothing. Joists, planks, doors and windows were all foraged. The shed is insulated and quite warm in winter.

Tim began his working life as an apprentice at a stone carving yard. He then moved on to the City and Guilds of London Art School, which was a place that still taught students in the traditional manner. 'I don't know how I got in there,' observes Tim, 'I hadn't done a single drawing. While there I got to do wood carving, stone carving, gilding, history of furniture, heraldry, lettering and many other subjects. I eventually became an assistant to one of the old boys who was a tutor at the School, and I used to help him at Westminster Abbey in re-carving worn statues, which I thought was pretty bloody wonderful for a young student! It wasn't strictly original work – mostly it was replacing faces and hands on statues which had become distressed by age and weather.' When Tim eventually retired from carving, he learnt how to do sports and remedial massage, 'It was still work where you used your hands, so I found it satisfying. It's just a change from wood or stone to human flesh.' Tim has always worked with his hands, so he likes to have projects on the go. He is presently restoring an old boat on the Essex coast, a work of love and passion.

Most of the roof is covered with corrugated plastic sheets enabling plenty of top light into the interior. In autumn, being under trees, the shed becomes a bit darker after leaf-fall. That's also when some maintenance is required.

The timber frame sits upon concrete flagstones laid on sand. Outside, the walls are feather-edge boards, whilst inside the lining is of plywood with insulation in between.

These are side-hung casements painted, as is the rest of the shed, with a mixture of preservative and old engine oil in order to keep out the elements.

The door is a second-hand panelled construction, painted to match the rest of the shed.

Tim has two goats in the small field in front of his shed. The animals wander about quite freely, and often enter the shed when Tim is in there working. They are inquisitive animals. Tim rather likes the fact that the goats take more of an interest in what he's doing than most humans!

CHAINSAW SHED

David recalls that his interest in carving began when he was a teenager; he carved a broom handle with a fist and arm at its end. He found it relatively easy, so he went on and carved some other things, all of which gave him a great deal of satisfaction. However, David's career took him in another direction, and he joined the police cadets at age sixteen. Following a successful career as a police officer, he eventually retired from the force, and his love of carving once again came to the fore. He remembers seeing a wood-carver working with a chainsaw in a layby and was intrigued that such work could be done so skilfully.

David trained as a tree-surgeon and learnt how to use chainsaws professionally. He did this for some years but it didn't fully satisfy his need for carving, but the job did provide him with free wood for his wood-burner! Eventually, he met Dennis (with whom he works) who introduced him to chainsaw carving. 'I do like the freedom,' says David, 'and the quiet contemplation or solitude that you get when you are working in the open. You get completely absorbed in your work. I must say that I do look at a lot of art: paintings and sculpture. I try to understand what the artist is trying to convey with his work. It's fascinating for me; I suppose I have come to carve wood rather later in life, but, nonetheless I enjoy every moment. The smell, the feel, the surprise when you find an unexpected grain in the middle of the wood: it all gives me a lot of joy and a feeling of accomplishment.'

The shed was bought from eBay and, using a borrowed trailer, was transported rather precariously to its present site at the edge of a wood. The building sits harmoniously under an old hornbeam pollard. The walls are strongly made from pine and the outside is of lapped boards. To prevent water ingress, a breather lining is added to the back of the boards. The whole building is stained with preservative.

The roof construction is of A-trusses with T&G boards fixed to the latter. The outside covering is of the usual roofing felt. There is no gutter so that the rainwater is just discharged onto the ground.

Rather plain windows let light into the building. Some are top-hinged opening lights, but, as the shed door is always open, there is plenty of light inside.

The door is of the braced board construction typical of such sheds.

The interior is very cosy. A wood-burning stove has been added which gives warmth and dryness to the shed. It can also be used to keep food warm. As the building is rather isolated, a generator is used intermittently when electricity is needed for lighting on dark winter days. Of course, the setting is wonderful, at the edge of the wood. In the evening, pheasants and other poultry wander about scratching among the sawdust. Altogether a very tranquil place.

SHED OF CURIOUS THINGS

Clive moved to his present home over ten years ago, and inherited the shed. At the time, it was very run-down and leaked. After quite a lot of repair work, Clive managed to get the shed into working order. he added guttering and collected the rainwater; he lagged the interior so that he could work there in winter; and painted the outside an attractive shade of autumn sky.

Clive is a man of many talents: designer, musician, artist, collector of found objects, welder, lighting designer, and so on. He taught himself to weld so that he could join pieces of metal, old pipes, keys, tools, etc. and make these into interesting sculptural forms. The garden surrounding the shed is full of surprises – like strings of flints moving gently in the wind.

'I was always into recycling,' observes Clive. 'As a child I used to bring home all sorts of objects I had found – much to my mother's disgust. Even now, I cannot walk past a skip without first checking if anything in it could be useful. My friends who like sheds absolutely love mine, but others just think I am a crazy hoarder! I have a few close friends with whom I share a so-called "shed night" – that's when we get together in our shed and drink beer and light bonfires! We take it in turns.'

The walls are plain lapped boards on a timber frame. The inside has been lagged with Rockwool and plywood in order to preserve heat, and to stop the interior getting too hot in summer.

The roof is made of roofing felt discharging into PVC guttering. The water is collected into some interesting and unusual containers. Even the downpipes are odd.

The windows are quite small but just about let in enough light for close work to be done. There is power and light in the shed.

The shed door is made of vertical boards on a simple frame. Clive has maximized the storage potential on the back of the door with all sorts of hooks and screws, from which hang a variety of useful household tools and objects.

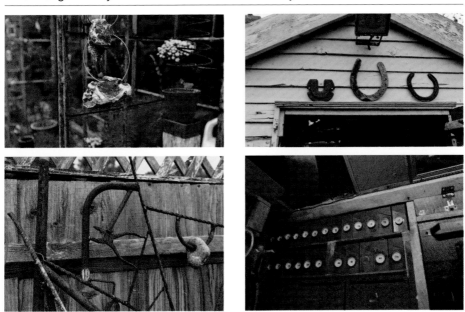

Clive is a creative individual and his fertile mind has come up with some wonderful solutions to problems, such as using the inside of beer bottle tops to identify storage boxes, or funny little handles on cupboards. Even the downpipe collecting the rainwater is made of an old flexible vacuum cleaner hose. Recycling in practice!

DEVELOPMENT SHED

Garrett built his shed in 2004, and has recorded the fact in the concrete floor. There had been no shed in the garden prior to that, so that Garrett was able to start from scratch. He designed the structure and made a sturdy timber frame. The outside was clad in feather-edge board; something he now regrets doing. He thinks it might have been better to have clad the outer surface with shiplap – an altogether stronger and more durable surface. Similarly the roof, which is made from corrugated clear PVC to allow a lot of light into the interior, also allows a lot of condensation inside, which is not good.

In winter the shed does tend to get a bit cold, as standing on a concrete floor drains the body heat away. Garrett did try carpet offcuts, but swarf gets stuck in the piles and it's almost impossible to remove. Someone suggested a wooden slatted panel, but Garrett thinks that too would prove hazardous as he'd be tripping up all the time. The winter damp also creates rust on the metal surfaces, so the shed is not quite perfect yet. Many of Garrett's ideas are 'in development' so to speak, so it's very likely that the shed is in its development phase, and will no doubt be improved in the future. Problems are there to be solved.

Garrett wanted the walls to be strong, so he built the frame from big tanalised timbers. The joints are joined together in a variety of different ways; metal fishplates, brackets, screws etc. Externally the walls are of treated feather-edge boards.

The roof covering is of translucent, corrugated PVC sheets nailed to timber rafters. In order to prevent condensation falling onto his bench and tools, Garrett has slid hardboard under the corrugated sheets.

There are no windows as such: light enters from above via the roof.

The doorway has double doors. Garrett has devised a very unusual system of door-stay. Made completely of timber and rope, both doors have the same method of being held open in summer.

The shed is virtually hidden from view by trees, bushes and other small buildings at the foot of the garden. It is a charming refuge in which Garrett can develop ideas and make things. He likes to have a problem that he can try to solve, sometimes even having to learn a new skill (such as plastic forming) in the process. He wishes the building was a bit larger, but at least the small size forces him to be tidy!

LA CABANE

The shed was originally an asbestos garage when Sean moved to the property. It had not been used for many years and was in a poor and neglected state. Sean wanted a warm, cosy interior so he set about making an insulated concrete floor slab, battening and cladding the exterior and lining the internal walls, also heavily insulated. To complete the picture, a wood-burning stove was added. According to Sean, 'You only need to burn a few sticks for an hour or so and that's enough to keep the interior warm and toasty! It's a bit too big – the stove that is – for the building, but it's one of those things you find out after you've put it in. I have also realized something else: the space is not big enough. I really need two sheds, one for working in and one for storage. I got one thing right though – everything in here is on wheels, so I can move things around.' The door has an interesting porthole in it. Apparently Sean finished building a large boat some years ago and the porthole was 'surplus to requirements' so it was re-used in the shed, making a distinctive looking shed door. He had to line the inside face to make the job perfect, but that was a relatively easy task for Sean who is experienced in the use of plastics.

The outside is feather-edge boards heavily treated with tanalising solution to keep out the weather. Inside Sean has used the cheapest, but strong and rigid, OSB board and painted that with emulsion. Rockwool insulation lines the inside and the original asbestos corrugated walls are trapped within, undisturbed.

The roof is of the original corrugated asbestos, which will be replaced one day. Rainwater is not collected and falls directly onto the garden.

There are very good windows on two sides as Sean likes to make models and build things, which needs maximum daylight.

The original door was a plain, braced and ledged door. The porthole distinguishes and makes it unique. The inside has been lined with insulation and MDF. It is important for Sean to be able to see the house from the shed, so that he knows when tea is ready!

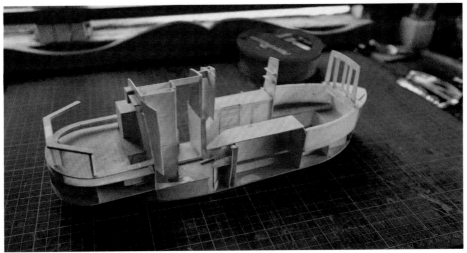

Sean spends many hours peacefully in his shed, making models or just listening to the radio and watching the bird life in his garden. The interior of the shed is very well fitted out. There is a swing-away seat which sits neatly under the work-top; the gaps between the OSB boards have a batten covering (and the screw-hole pitch has been carefully measured). Everything is neat and orderly. Sean is very particular about doing things properly and takes great pride in his workmanship, as every craftsman should.

HMS SUMMERHOUSE

Ray is a most unusual engineer: everything he tackles is done in an unconventional, but very practical, way. There was a pond in the property when he moved in, but he enlarged it a bit more in order to accommodate a large concrete plinth. He then constructed a steel frame which overhangs the island so that one gets a feeling of being afloat. As Ray says, 'I wanted to feel isolated in a very real way, and having my shed on an island seemed to be the best way to do that. Also, having the verandah allowed me to just sit there in winter – there's more than enough heat generated by the wood stove – or summer, and watch the chickens or the cats play.' Not many outsiders are invited into the shed; it's mostly inhabited by Ray and one cat. Apart from being a retreat, the shed is used to store tools, screws and other detritus of a working life – the stove is lit during cold weather, so there is never a problem with rusty tools, which Ray (and every craftsman worth his salt) hates.

The pond sits under several trees, so it's a bit of a problem to keep it clean. Surplus rainwater is fed back into the pond, and a small fountain oxygenates the water so that frogs and other small creatures can thrive.

The shed walls have a metal frame and this is clad with boards obtained cheaply from a second-hand source. There is no insulation within the walls, but the wood is naturally warm.

Ray wanted to minimize cutting so the roof is covered by standard 8x4 ft plywood boards, the overhangs from which provide cover for the verandah. Roofing felt is fixed to the ply. Water is collected via large guttering feeding into a 1000-litre butt; any surplus goes into the pond.

There are no windows as this would reduce interior space. One porthole in the door lets in a little light, but, as Ray is an electrical engineer, the interior space is well catered for in the lighting department.

The door is a purpose-built stable door, the upper part having a porthole with a complicated locking system.

The shed is occasionally used as a base when having a party, for instance, on 5 November when there's a bonfire. It's a useful refuge against falling skyrockets, and it's warm. Ray has sometimes slept in the shed. His dad's old air rifle hangs above the stove as a reminder of family fun; he never uses it for shooting. The shed is a wonderful place, especially when it's raining hard: the sound of falling torrents makes a soothing companion to the warm wood stove.

THE CONSTRUCTION

When asked about a name for his shed, Victor replies 'It's called "The Construction" and I think it's been here a good twenty to twenty-five years. It came about because my brother-in-law used to be a tipper lorry driver. He used to work for local councils, and the plastic sheets literally fell off the back of a lorry when the wagon carrying them shed its load into the road. My brother-in-law was asked to go and clear up the mess, so he took the sheets to the council yard. The owners of the sheets didn't want them anymore, and the council didn't want them, so I ended up with them. I think that someone said the sheets were originally the surface of a roller skating rink. I had been thinking of building a shed and the sheets were like manna from heaven – I could use them for the walls. Luckily, the bungalow was being converted into a two storey building, so I used the old joists and rafters as the frame for this shed.'

Victor was a bit worried that the shed, which is quite large, would be too much of an eyesore, so he planted wisteria along the wall which is visible from the house. This has now grown up along the wall and over the roof and looks very pretty when the blossom is out.

The frame is of second-hand pine timbers reclaimed from the bungalow modifications. Cladding is of 20 mm thick translucent white plastic. No-one is certain exactly what it is, but it lets light in. There is no insulation. The shed has a substantial concrete base, hand cast by its owner.

The original roof was of corrugated asbestos which was reclaimed from a disused site. Gradually that fractured in places, so Victor has covered the gaps with corrugated iron sheets, again salvaged from a dump. The rainwater just drains off one side onto the garden.

Even the doors are made of the same plastic as the walls. This makes them quite heavy, so strong hinges were needed. Unfortunately the doors have warped and cracked quite a bit over the years, but Victor has repaired them.

Curiously for a building of this size there are no windows. All the light comes in through the translucent walls.

It's a rather odd building, this shed, sited in a large garden which has several other sheds. Some are pre-formed plastic from a garden centre. Some are conventional timber sheds. Then there is this milky-white construction, looking very mysterious and not like a building at all. It has the air of a space-ship that has just landed, apart from the established wisteria.

DONATELLO SHED

Joe and his wife Valerie decided that they needed a shed some years ago. They needed somewhere for Joe to keep his tools and store bicycles and, as Valerie keeps bees, somewhere dry for bee-keeping equipment. They decided to buy a shed from a reputable manufacturer in kit form. It was duly assembled and pretty soon filled up. There was already a garage on the site, dating back to the early thirties, but it was far too small for storage. That's why the new shed was bought.

Joe is a gentle, quiet man, a sculptor and musician. Pieces of his work are strewn around inside and outside the shed. It's very difficult to find enough space in which to create new work as the shed is quite full as it is. When Valerie and Joe first moved into the house, Joe needed to have a workshop, somewhere within which he could make things and which had a vice and a bench. The shed was bought for speed and efficiency, otherwise Joe would have probably constructed his own shed from scratch.

Asked if he allows other people into his shed, Joe replies 'Well, there is a dart board in the shed! You'd have trouble finding it though, as anyone who has tried to squeeze in there will tell you. No, there's not enough space really.'

The shiplap boards which form the outer skin are typical of a shed of this type, which is factory-made to a specific design. The timbers are treated with preservative stain.

The roofing felt, single-pitch roof discharges rainwater into PVC guttering and downpipes down to a water butt. The water is collected and used for the garden.

There are many windows for such a small building, some of which are opening casements. Joe particularly wanted a lot of light so that he could work on his art pieces.

A timber stable door allows access to the front face of the shed, but in addition a pair of large garage doors in one face permits large objects to be brought in and out of the shed.

Joe and Valerie are keen conservationists and try to grow their own vegetables in the back garden. Chickens are allowed to roam wherever they wish, even though a few vegetables get scratched out. Valerie keeps bees and makes honey. Were it not for the house, the back garden, with its collection of sheds, vegetables and chickens, could easily be an allotment by any other name.

POTTING SHED

Gail is very interested in advertising, graphics and signs. When she came across the sign marked 'Potting Shed' she could not resist buying it and putting it up on her own shed. The building was put up by a specialist manufacturer on a substantial concrete base over fifteen years ago. Originally intended as a small workshop and store when Gail was dabbling in repairing and restoring antiques as a hobby, the antiques were gradually phased out in favour of art as she became more interested in producing artworks. The shed is quite large, occupying most of the width of the garden.

Gail is very happy for other people to visit her shed. She adds, 'I did toy with the idea of having "workshops" in my workshop! But I went off that and concentrated on developing my techniques. I came rather late to the business of art, but I'm very excited by this whole new world; I can't get enough of it.'

When Gail was a baby it was common practice for mothers to put their babies outside 'in the fresh air' as it was considered good for them. Her mum did just that. When the weather was bad, Gail (in her pram) was put into the family shed. She thinks her love of sheds and their spaces stems from those early memories. As Gail recalls, 'It's hard to describe in words, but I've always loved the smell of sheds.'

Externally the walls are of treated shiplap boards. The internal walls have been lined with plywood by Gail's dad. There is extensive insulation throughout.

The roof is a double pitch covered in roofing felt. The gutters drain into PVC downpipes, allowing the rainwater to be collected in butts for use in the garden. Inside, the ceiling is lined with white melamine-faced hardboard with Rockwool inside.

Several windows in two walls allow a lot of light into the interior, making the inside very bright and airy.

Double, partially-glazed doors give wide access to the shed. This is especially important for access when Gail is carrying large works of art.

Although the shed is not unusual in any way, it provides a warm and quiet haven for making art pieces – a true refuge from the everyday trials and tribulations of life.

OLD GARDEN SHED

Tom lives in a Georgian house and reckons that the shed at the foot of his garden is contemporaneous with the house. The shed fits neatly into a corner having two old brick garden walls as part of its construction. Many repairs have been carried out by Tom over the course of his lifetime to the walls, tiles, rafters and windows. At one time, the garden wall fronting the road was leaning over in danger of collapse – it would have pulled the shed into the road with it. Tom rebuilt the garden wall so that it was vertical and saved the shed.

Tom's dad had a transport and haulage business, using horses at the time, in London Colney. Tom recalls times when he was little when his dad used horses and carts to go into London, taking hay feed and bringing out manure for the farms.

Tom and his dad loved the horses. As he recalls, 'We had this great, big old cart-horse, Jolly. Well, he had enormous legs with fluffy feathers at the hoof. Jolly was quite a jumpy horse and he wouldn't let people near him, apart from Dad. But he seemed to like me – and I liked him. Whenever I could, I used to sneak into the stable and cuddle his legs, and he used to let me. Stood there all quiet with me hugging his legs. I was only little, say two or three years old then. One day, when Jolly was being stabled in a pub nearby, my parents lost me. They looked about and found me in Jolly's stable, holding his leg!'

The old walls are of 230 mm hand-made brick, built with lime mortar. Inside, there is old lime plaster which has been whitewashed many times.

The roof is of a single pitch covered by hand-made, local clay tiles. These are hung with tile pegs over battens fixed to rafters. There is no lining to the underside, so that all the construction is visible.

The original timber windows were in a bad state of repair, so Tom had a local joiner make up some new windows and frames which have been painted to look very smart.

A simple plank door is braced and ledged and painted a modest grey colour, fitting in very well with the mellow brick walls and nearby planting.

Undoubtedly the best feature of this little building is its snug fit into the corner of the garden. As it forms part of the boundary wall, the shed sits there like a worn and much-loved old shoe.

After 300 years or so it has seen many owners come and go. Tom is very fond of it.

THE WHITE SHED

Roy found this shed in bits, abandoned by an old hedge. The owner dismantled the old shed into its respective panels, and leant it outside his house. Never being one to waste materials, Roy acquired ownership and put up the building in his garden some thirty years ago.

Roy has been a stuntman for most of his life. He began his career as a skating gymnast appearing in ice shows all over the world. Eventually, he ended up in Hollywood. Roy has worked with many stars of the silver screen, including John Wayne, Roger Moore, Sean Connery, Harrison Ford, etc. His list of film credits reads like a who's who of post-war cinema greats.

Recently, Roy was at an exhibition in London where he re-acquainted himself with Brian Blessed. As Roy observes, 'We worked together on *Flash Gordon* – that had Sam Jones playing Flash. I was one of the Hawkmen doing flying stunts in a very cold sound stage. We were freezing up in the gods, so I asked one of the runners to get some heat in. They produced some industrial heaters and pretty quickly, instead of freezing we were sweating and the make-up and wax was running off us. It was like Icarus all over again!'

Roy, a life-long sun-worshipper, dressed as a naturist cowboy!

The roofing felt had some holes in it so another layer of felt was added over the old felt and held down along the edges by roofing battens. Below the eaves of the front gable, roofing felt has been tucked over the edge and held down by a roofing batten nailed onto the walls. It stops the wind getting under the felt and ripping it off. Practical, but not beautiful.

Poor detailing along the windows led to the sill rotting away years ago. It has been replaced by a batten screwed along the window frame.

Although the shed has a slight 'lean' to starboard, it's been a very important item in Roy's life. In it he has put together bits of kit for stunts, worked out various schemes for new games ideas, and stored his tools and bikes.

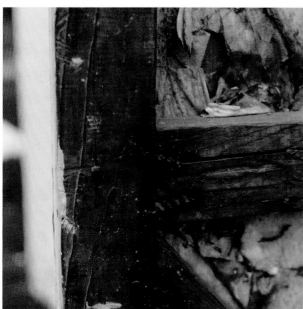

The bottom of the front door was rotten. With some surplus roofing felt, a batten, and a few clout nails the holes were stopped up. It may look messy, but it's been keeping the water out for over thirty years. The corrugated fixings holding the rails and braces on the inside of the front door have long been rusty. It's the fastest and cheapest way of holding two pieces of wood together, though it would make any craftsman shudder. Note the so-called 'insulation'.

SEWING SHED

Ulrike has had her shed for over twenty years. In it, she has taught many students the craft of sewing and clothes-making. She used to do her sewing in the main house but found that it was impossible to leave her things lying about when visitors came or when small children visited. A separate building was the ideal solution. The shed was supplied and assembled by a company that specialized in small buildings, and lined inside with insulation and panelled with hardboard.

Although Ulrike spends a lot of time working on her own in the shed, friends are allowed to visit her there as well as students. She also has a radio for company, and the interior is warm and de-humidified (because of the steam iron).

Ulrike began needle-working in Germany with a three-year apprenticeship. When the Second World War broke out, she went to live with some relations in Switzerland where it was safer. After a period there she moved again, this time to the UK. She moved from Yorkshire, to Lancashire, to Surrey, and so on, each time bringing her sewing machine with her for, as she notes, 'Swiss sewing machines are built to last forever; I would never leave my beloved sewing machine behind.'

The basic shed is built on a concrete base and a frame with shiplap boards on the outside. The entire building is insulated and lined with oil-tempered hardboard, which is left unpainted internally.

The roof is covered by roofing felt and is of a single pitch. Rainwater is collected into a water butt for use in the garden.

Most of the south-facing wall is made up of windows, with some opening casements. Ulrike's work table needs maximum light which is why the shed is orientated this way.

The simple braced and ledged door is typical of almost every shed, except that this one is lined inside.

Ulrike is very proud of her teaching. As she says 'I want to pass on my knowledge. My adult students are wonderful. They want to come; they want to learn – and they have patience. I have taught students with learning difficulties. It is so satisfying when they get so much out of learning to sew. Sometimes, a piece of work takes weeks but then you have something which is your own.'

CHAPEL OF EASE

The materials for Cally's shed came from a nearby chapel. According to Cally, 'It was a shame the chapel got pulled down, otherwise I would have bought it. It was a Bolton and Paul kit chapel – the sort which used to get sent out to Africa with the missionaries – and the corrugated iron was just what I needed for building my shed.'

Although the shed is used like most sheds for contemplation, storage, etc., it now houses an outside toilet. Cally recalls the exciting 'frisson' of having a poo in the open air as a boy. The excitement of using outdoor facilities, well away from the house, is still attractive. The sounds of night-time; the rain on the tin roof; the spiders making their webs inside the shed; all of these are pleasures which are not to be found in an indoor toilet. Sometimes Cally likes to sit and think, sometimes just to sit – either way, it's always a pleasure.

As a gesture to the original chapel and its use, the shed has many items of religious memorabilia, which makes it a rather special place for pondering on the frenetic pace of the outside world. The name given to the building hints at Cally's unusual, and always original, sense of humour.

The timber frame is of second-hand timbers sourced locally, while the walls are clad in galvanized, corrugated iron from the ex-chapel. Some patches of rust are showing, but it all adds to the shed's rural charm.

The roof is exactly the same construction as the walls, giving the building a homogenous look.

There is one small window, which is an opening casement. An old lace curtain adds a small touch of privacy.

The door has been made from old tongue-and-groove planks. The hinges were made specially for the job.

The charm of this shed-chapel is partly in its setting – hidden as it is among the trees and foliage – and partly due to its fittings and ornaments. The sink is made out of an old army ammo box. The wooden planks are all from previous existences. The religious artefacts give a clue to the uninitiated.

VERANDAH SHED

Barry has always been interested in woodwork. His two former sheds were quickly outgrown, so he decided to build himself a grander, more spacious building complete with sitting area from which he could contemplate the world. He loves cabinet-making so his work-bench is very smart. It has drawers with dovetailed joints and an edged and laminated top, but this soon got covered with stuff.

Barry began his career working with livestock, moving on to transportation and working with Portakabins. One day he noticed that one of these buildings was being demolished. Quick to spot an opportunity, Barry managed to obtain the plywood floor sections for nothing. This more or less decided the size of the new shed that he had been thinking about building.

Gradually, all of the various joists and beams were found from various sites until Barry eventually had enough materials to begin work. The ground level in his garden slopes towards the house so the first thing Barry had to do was to build brick piers with the help of a friend. Most of the walls not visible from the house are clad with old billboard plywood sections, while the visible sides are shiplap boards. Even these were sourced second-hand. Apparently, the most expensive part of the building is the roofing felt. Apart from that just about everything, including the lights, is foraged or donated.

Half of the shed is clad in old plywood, and the other in shiplap boards. The frame is made from old joists, insulated with Rockwool. The floor is made of sections from an old Portakabin and sits on heavy beams resting on brick piers.

The roof is made in the same way as the walls from second-hand plywood on old rafters. It is insulated inside.

These are old pre-formed windows from a Portakabin, given free for the project. They don't open, but Barry doesn't worry about that as long as he has enough light to work by.

Barry made the stable door. He can have the upper section open without allowing his dog to wander in. The extra ventilation is useful when working in a dusty environment.

The shed sits at the back of the garden amongst the usual debris and clutter found in just about any garden. Barry likes to work on several projects at a time. He has made cabinets, tables, chests and so on for most of his family. He loves to work with wood, and is happiest when he is making something in his shed. His dry sense of humour is evident from the various signs around. It's a happy place.